Cruise the Danube Nuremberg to Budapest

DRMW

Cover Photograph

Dürnstein

For my wife

Copyright remains for DRMW 20 October 2019.

Other e-books by the author (available from Amazon Kindle)

UNITED KINGDOM

Complete Butterflies of the UK and Ireland.

Landscapes of Borrowdale and Buttermere.

Wildflowers of the UK and Ireland.

FLORIDA

A Photographic Guide to Common Butterflies of Southern Florida.

Some Common Birds of Florida, A Pictorial Guide.

TURKEY and GREECE

Turkey Aegean Coast, Landscapes and Natural History around Teos and Sigacik.

Wildflowers and Landscapes of The Peloponnese.

Common Wildflowers and Butterflies of Greece.

The Orchids of Rhodes.

Common Orchids of Crete.

GERMANY

Cruise on the Middle Rhine and Moselle, a photoguide.

Cruise the Waterways in Holland.

Cruise Medieval Germany, Nuremberg to Mainz.

PORTUGAL

Cruise the Douro

ASIA

Vietnam and Cambodia, Wild Life and Landscapes.

Kerala, Landscapes and Natural History.

Butterflies of Sri Lanka, an illustrated checklist.

CANARY ISLANDS

Lanzarote, a Tour Guide, Wildflowers, Butterflies and Birds.

La Gomera Landscapes, Flora and Fauna.

La Palma a Photoguide and Wildflowers.

Fuerteventura a Photoguide & Wildflowers.

Flowers of the Canary Isles.

SINGAPORE and MALAYSIA

Singapore, Flowers Butterflies and Birds.

The Wildlife of Langkawi.

AUSTRALIA

The Eastern Goldfields of Western Australia.

Daisies and the Asteraceae of Western Australia.

Fanflowers and other Goodeniaceae of Western Australia.

Banksia, Grevillea and the other Proteaceae of Western Australia.

Common Butterflies of Western Australia.

Peas and Acacias of Western Australia.

Birds of Western Australia.

Kangaroo Paws and Coneflowers of Western Australia.

The Triggerplants of Western Australia.

An Introduction to Common Orchids of Western Australia.

Wildflowers of Western Australia.

Common Birds of Australia, Queensland and Northern Territory.

The Daintree, Birds and Butterflies.

Monsignor Hawes, Priest and Architect in Western Australia.

MUSIC

SCHUBERT The Songs of Goethe for the Listener An interactive e-Book.

BEETHOVEN String and Piano Quartets and Trios For the Listener An interactive e-Book.

MOZART String Chamber Music for the Listener An interactive e-Book.

Music in the Air, Elgar's 90, the stories of Opus 1 to Opus 90.

Edward Elgar, The Choral works and songs.

Kol Nidrei, The history of a song and a prayer.

Table of Contents

Nuremberg 11

Regensburg 37

Stolpersteines 48

Gunter Demnig 51

Passau 56

Salzburg 62

Schloss Leopoldskron 74

The Salzburg Festival 76

Linz 77

Melk 86

Dürnstein 104

Vienna 114

Bratislava 140

The Holocaust Memorial, Bratislava 166

Neologická synagogue, Bratislava 167

Budapest 172

The Shoes Memorial on the Danube Bank 182

Introduction

The Cruise that this book illustrates travels through four countries, Germany, Austria, Slovakia and Hungary.

This book is intended for the use of tourists enjoying a boat cruise on The Rhine–Main–Danube Canal and the Danube between Nuremberg and Budapest. The book describes the places that can be visited in this region and is amply illustrated with photographs.

For many of the cities visited on this cruise a large book would be required to describe all the sights available for the tourist. To keep the size of the publication and the sale price within reasonable limits it is not feasible to enter into an in depth account on each city stop.

Where the tourist requires more details on the sights visited it is advised that a detailed tour book is used to supplement this book. The book, like the cruise itself, is a taster for the visits to the cities that are described. Following the cruise, the tourist may well be encouraged to make a separate visit to places seen during the river cruise.

This book describes the sights that could be encountered in a brief visit made during a river cruise, a visit usually of a few hours, sometimes of a day or two, in such places. Where the author thought it was necessary, some historical background is given relating to WW2 and the places visited.

Many tourist companies run this industry river cruising in Europe using luxury boats with fine furnishings, well-equipped cabins with patio windows and excellent quality food and wine. You may even get an invitation to dine with the captain table at his table. Some companies even provide a balcony for the cabin.

Nuremberg

Nuremberg stands on the Rhine–Main–Danube Canal in the German state of Bavaria. The population of Nuremberg is in the region of 500,000. The city dates from the beginning of the 11th century. It became an important city of the Holy Roman Empire, one of the territories subordinate to the Holy Roman Emperor. This period of the Holy Roman Empire became known as the First Reich (962-1806), the Second Reich the period of the German Empire (1871-1918 and also onwards to 1933) and the Third Reich was the period of the Nazi regime (1933-1945).

Nuremberg was involved in many massacres. In 1298, the Jews of the town were accused of having desecrated the host and 698 of them were killed in a series of massacres. Again in 1349 Nuremberg's Jews were subjected to a pogrom. They were burned at the stake or expelled. Between 1349 and 1534, a period known as the plague years, many massacres of the Jews occurred.

Nuremberg became important to the Nazi Party when commencing in 1927 huge rallies were held in the city until 1938 (The Nuremberg Rallies). These were huge propaganda events (some of these were filmed) held at the Nazi party rally grounds, 11 square kilometres in the southeast of Nuremberg.

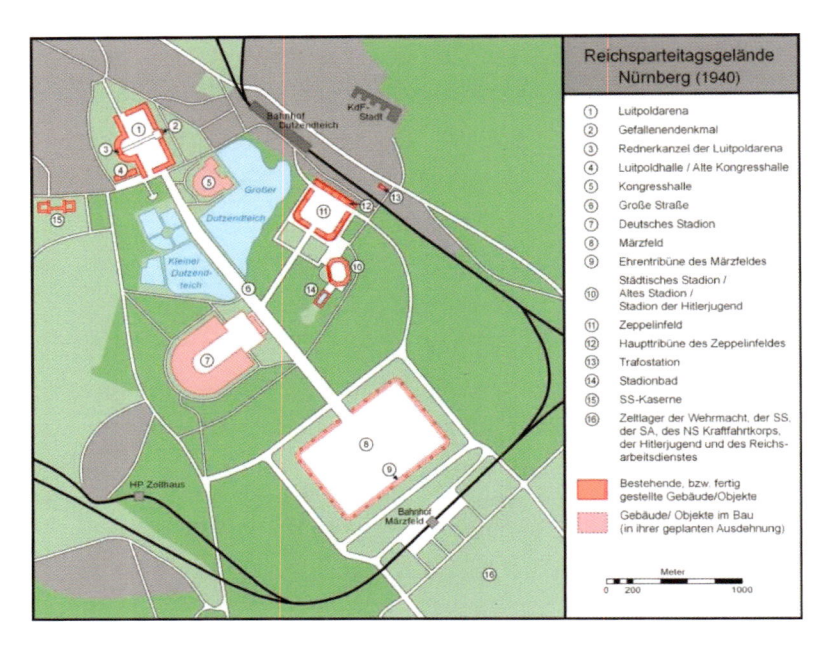

Map of the Nazi party rally grounds in Nuremberg in 1940

Image by Lencer Wikicommons images Creative Commons Attribution-Share Alike 2.5 Generic license.

Rally on The Zeppelin Fields, Nuremberg 1937

Image German federal Archives Wikicommons images Creative Commons Attribution-Share Alike 3.0 Germany license.

Between 1943 and 1945 Nuremberg sustained severe damage from Allied Forces strategic bombing. This also resulted in massive loss by the invading forces. Seven hundred planes participated. One hundred and six were shot down when returning to their bases. Over 700 men were missing, over 500 of them died and 160 became prisoners of war. On 2 January 1945 the medieval city centre of Nuremberg was heavily bombed by the Royal Air Force and the U.S. Army Air Forces. Within one hour 90 % was destroyed along with loss of homes and loss of life. A further attack took place in February 1945. In April 1945 the city was captured by infantry with further destruction of buildings.

The city was rebuilt after the war with reconstruction of some of the medieval buildings.

Nuremberg 1945

Image in the public domain Wikicommons images.

The Tribune Stand, Zeppelin Field, Nuremberg

This was the landing site of an airship in August 1909 carrying Ferdinand Graf von Zeppelin and later became part of the Nazi party rally grounds. The Zeppelin Field is now used for sport. The whole complex is preserved (along with many other Nazi sites) so that Germany will never forget what happened.

Congress Hall and The Dutzendteich Lake, Nuremberg

Up to one million members of the Nazi party would travel to Nuremberg for a week-long rally. The Congress Hall was commissioned by Hitler to hold over 50,000 people. It marked the entrance of the rally grounds. The building was never completed. In the north wing there is now an exhibition centre relating to Nazi Germany.

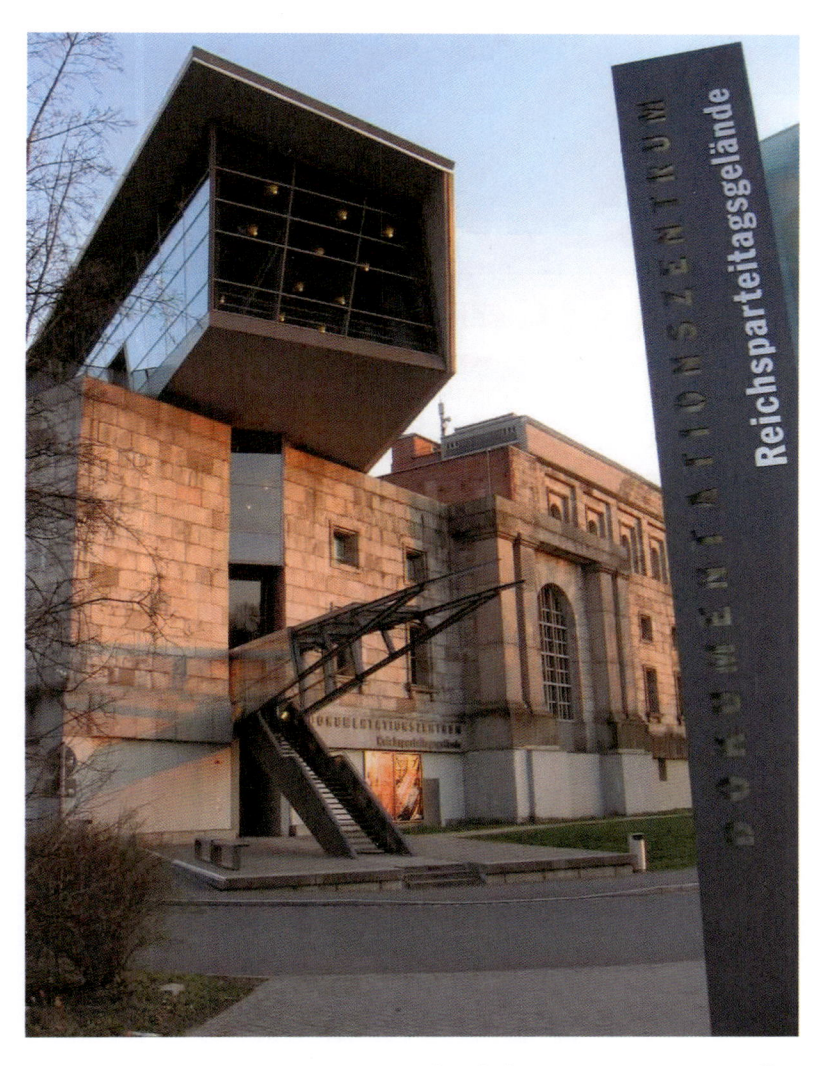

The Documentation Centre and Exhibition, Congress Hall

Image by Chris Baier Wikicommons images Creative Commons Attribution-Share Alike 2.5 Generic license.

Nazi War Crimes Tribunal

The Nuremberg Trials of officials who committed war crimes and crimes against humanity took place between 1945 and 1949. The site of the trials was chosen as Nuremberg for its symbolic value in the demise of the Nazi regime. Here the laws stripping Jews of their citizenship were passed. The trials took place in the Palace of Justice, which had largely survived war damage. This had a large court room that was enlarged for the trials. Adjacent was a large prison building.

International Military Tribunal trial of war criminals in Nuremberg,

Image in the public domain Wikicommons images

Palace of Justice, Nuremberg

Image by Magnus Gertkemper Wikicommons images Creative Commons Attribution-Share Alike 3.0 Unported license.

Anti-Semitic and Nuremberg Laws

From 1933 the Nazis began to implement their policies based on race. There was a national boycott of Jewish businesses, non-Aryans were barred from the legal profession and civil service. Books considered un-German, including those by Jewish authors, were destroyed in a nationwide book burning. Jewish citizens were harassed and subjected to violent attacks. They were actively suppressed, stripped of their citizenship and civil rights, and eventually completely removed from German society.

The Nuremberg anti-Semitic and racial laws dated from 1935. They were formed at the annual Nazi rally. The two laws were the Law for the Protection of German Blood and German Honour, which forbade marriages and extramarital intercourse between Jews and Germans and the employment of German females under 45 in Jewish households; and the Reich Citizenship Law, which declared that only those of German or related blood were eligible to be Reich citizens; the remainder were classed as state subjects, without citizenship rights. Prosecutions under the two laws did not commence until after the 1936 Summer Olympics.

Persons convicted of violating the marriage laws were imprisoned, and upon completing their sentences were re-arrested by the Gestapo and sent to Nazi concentration camps. Non-Jews gradually stopped socialising with Jews or shopping in Jewish-owned stores, many of which closed due to lack of customers. Jews were no longer permitted to work in the civil service or government-regulated professions such as medicine and education. They were forced to take menial employment. Emigration was problematic, as Jews were required to remit up to 90 per cent of their wealth as a tax upon leaving the country. In mid-1941, the German government started mass exterminations of the Jews of Europe.

The Imperial Castle (Kaiserburg Castle), Nuremberg

The Imperial Castle

Image by KPFC Wikicommons images Creative Commons Attribution-Share Alike 3.0 Unported, 2.5 Generic, 2.0 Generic and 1.0 Generic license.

The medieval fortified buildings of The Imperial Castle lie on a sandstone ridge overlooking Nuremberg. They date from about the year 1000. In the middle ages it was used by Holy Roman Emperors. Later it was used by all German kings and emperors.

This was damaged in WW2 and has since been restored.

The Imperial Castle

Image by Hajo Dietz Wikicommons images Creative Commons Attribution-Share Alike 3.0 Unported license.

Church of Our Lady, (Frauenkirche), Nuremberg

Image by Kolossos Wikicommons Creative Commons Attribution-Share Alike 3.0 Unported license.

This Gothic church is in the main square. It dates from 1352. The church was built in the place of a former Jewish synagogue, which was destroyed during the pogrom of 1349.

Church of Our Lady (Frauenkirche)

Image by Diego Delso Wikicommons images Creative Commons Attribution-Share Alike 3.0 Unported license.

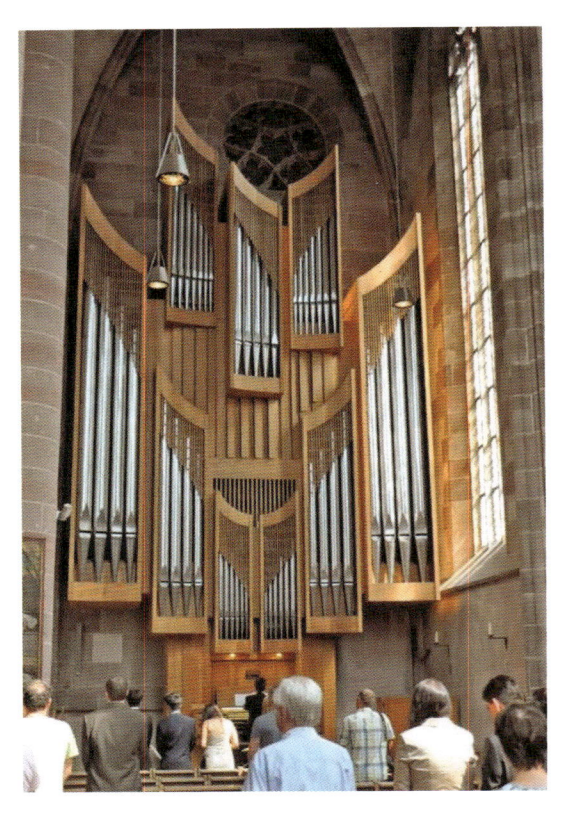

The Organ, Frauenkirche

Image by Hans-Jörg Gemeinholzer Wikicommons images Creative Commons Attribution-Share Alike 3.0 Germany license.

The organ was built in 1988 using elements from a previous instrument. The builders were the family business Orgelbau Klais that was founded in 1882. The business is run by the great-grandson of the founder. The company builds and restores organs worldwide. They also built the organ in the cathedral in Cologne.

The Männleinlaufen on Frauenkirche

The mechanical clock that commemorates the Golden Bull of 1356 dates from 1506. The Holy Roman Emperor is shown seated with the prince-electors surrounding him. At midday a bell rings and the sequence of rotating figures begins.

Church of St. Lawrence, (Lorenzkirche)

Image by jailbird Wikicommons Creative Commons Attribution-Share Alike 2.0 Germany license.

The church dates from 1400 and is built in the Gothic style. It has three organs. The interior contains the Angelic Salutation celebrating the Annunciation (1517-1518) by Veit Stoss. It is a church of the Evangelical Lutheran Church.

The Angelic Salutation

Image by Andreas Praefcke Wikicommons in the public domain.

German National Museum, Nuremberg

Image by Keichwa Wikicommons Creative Commons Attribution-Share Alike 3.0 Unported license.

The museum contains items relating to German culture and art from prehistoric times to the present day. It is Germany's largest museum of cultural history.

Nuremberg Fountain, (Schoner Brunnen), Nuremberg

This gothic structure stands in the main market square and is known as the Beautiful Fountain. It dates from the 14th century. It was built by the German Stonemason Heinrich Beheim.

Forty figures adorn the fountain. They represent the world view of the Holy Roman Empire. They are philosophy, the seven liberal arts, the four Evangelists, the four Church Fathers, the seven Prince-electors, the Nine Worthies, Moses and seven Prophets (Hosea, Daniel, Jeremiah, Ezekiel, Amos, Isaiah and Joel).

Old Town Hall, (Altes Rathaus), Nuremberg

This renaissance building, the Old Town Hall dates from the 16-17th century was rebuilt in the 1950s following severe war damage. The new town hall was also built in the 1950s.

Sculpture, The Ship of Fools, Nuremberg

This sculpture of a boat carrying seven people, a skeleton, and a dog is based on a sixteenth-century book by Sebastian Brant, this piece was sculpted by Juergen Weber. This gloomy sculpture shows an expelled Adam and Eve, their murderous son Cain and other violent figures.

Fleisch Bridge, Nuremberg

The Hangmans Flat and Bridge, Nuremberg

Image by Schlaier Wikicommons images Creative Commons Attribution-Share Alike 3.0 Unported, 2.5 Generic, 2.0 Generic and 1.0 Generic license.

Fronfeste (soccage-stronghold) and Kettensteg (chain-bridge), Nuremberg

Image by Tobias Bar Wikicommons the Creative Commons Attribution-Share Alike 2.0 Generic license.

It is at this site that the river Pegnitz leaves the old town through the city wall.

Regensburg

Regensburg stands at the confluence of the Danube, Naab and Regen rivers, where the Rhine-Main-Danube canal terminates after a course of 171 kms, passing Nuremberg on its way. Settlements here at Regensburg date from the stone age. The city has about 150,000 citizens.

The Regensburg Synagogue was destroyed on November 9, 1938, during Kristallnacht.

In WW2 Regensburg was home to both a Messerschmitt Bf 109 aircraft factory and an oil refinery. which were bombed by the Allies in 1943. The medieval city sustained little damage in the bombing.

The Stone Bridge, Regensburg

This bridge dates from about 1135, when it replaced a wooden bridge. It links the Old Town with Stadtamhof. Until the 1930s it was the only crossing of the Danube at Regensburg. The 17th-century Regensburg Salt Store and the Sausage Kitchen are adjacent to the bridge. The bridge has always caused difficulty for river traffic due to low height of the 16 arches. Originally having 3 towers, only the south tower, the city gate, survives.

The City Gate

This gate was destroyed by fire in the Thirty Years' War, when the city was under occupation by the Swedes. It was rebuilt in 1648 when the clock was added.

The legend of the bridge The bridge builder and the cathedral builder competed to find who would finish their work first. When the building of the cathedral progressed faster than that of the bridge, the bridge builder made a pact with the Devil. In exchange for the first three souls to cross the bridge, the Devil would help. The bridge was the first to be completed. Because of the pact with the Devil, the builder of the bridge sent a rooster, a hen and a dog across the bridge first instead of people. As a result, the enraged Devil made an unsuccessful attempt to destroy the bridge. It is said that this is the reason that the bridge has a bend in it.

St Peters Cathedral

Image Omnidoom 999 Wikipedia Creative Commons Attribution-Share Alike 2.5 Generic license.

St. Peters Roman Catholic church is a Gothic building. It dates from 1280 but the building did not open until 1520. Its present appearance with the two spires dates from 1869.

St Peters Cathedral

Image Jens Hirsch Wikipedia Creative Commons Attribution-Share Alike 3.0 Unported license.

Judensau

Image Bkmd Wikipedia in the public domain.

On the exterior of the cathedral there is a Judensau (Jews' sow), a stone carving of a sow and three Jews hanging onto its teats, a carving that mocks Judaism. These stone carvings are usually on the exterior of the building but on occasion can be found inside. The Judensau faces in the direction of the former Jewish quarter at the Neupfarrplatz. In Nazi Germany, classes of German schoolchildren were sent to see the Judensau on German churches. They are to be found in many churches in Germany, Austria and elsewhere in Europe. In some instances they have been removed.

Judensau across Europe

Image Lencer Creative Commons Attribution-Share Alike 3.0 Unported license.

The above map shows the sites of Judensau across Europe. Those marked in red have been removed.

Altes Rathaus, Regensburg

Image by Hajotthu Wikipedia Creative Commons Attribution-Share Alike 3.0 Unported license.

This still has an administrative function but is also home to Regensburg Museum. The building dates from 1320.

Colosseum Hotel

There were originally 225 Jews living in Regensburg. A number of these left Germany. Those that stayed were required to live in two buildings, one being an old person's home. Many who stayed were later sent to Theresienstadt.

During Kristallnacht in November 1938, local Nazis destroyed the Synagogue and the community centre. Jewish homes and stores and their contents were also destroyed. The Rabbi Salomon and his wife were forced out of their apartment and ordered to stand outside in their nightwear while their home was being demolished by the Nazis. By 1939, all the traders' and businessmen's property had been transferred to Christians.

In March 1944, a satellite labor camp of the Flossenbürg concentration camp was opened in the Colosseum Hotel in Regensburg. Four hundred and sixty males were imprisoned here, 150 of these males were Jews. Living conditions were extremely poor. In April 1945 the camp was cleared and inmates were sent on a death march to the south. Those that were unable to make this journey were killed. On May 3 1945 survivors on the march were liberated by US army troops.

Regensburg Synagogue in 1915

Image Wikipedia in the public domain.

Stolpersteines (stumbling stones) in honour of Jews deported during Nazism

Image Herbstlaub Wikipedia in the public domain

Stolpersteine or Stumbling stones

The small brass plaques (Stolpersteine or Stumbling stones) in the pavement in front of houses of which the (mostly Jewish) residents were persecuted or murdered by the Nazis, mention the name, date of birth and place (mostly a concentration camp) and date of death.

These and many other Stolpersteines in Germany, Austria, Hungary, the Netherlands, Belgium, the Czech Republic, Norway and Ukraine are by the artist Gunter Demnig. In 2017 one was set in Buenos Aires. The latter to commemorate children who were forced to flee Europe between 1933 and 1945. There number over 69,000 in about 2000 places in Europe with the project running since 1996. The brass plaques are laid into the pavement in front of their last address. With the numbers of the dead running into the millions Demnig makes the statement that the project is symbolic and it will never be possible to commemorate all the Nazi victims.

Gunter Demnig states from the Talmud that:

"A person is only forgotten when his or her name is forgotten".

(From the Gunter Demnig Website and with the kind permission of Gunter Demnig)

Gunter Demnig was born in Berlin in 1947. He studied art. He has received many awards for his work throughout Germany.

Gunter Demnig
Image by Sigismund von Dobschütz Wikicommons Creative Commons Attribution-Share Alike 3.0 Unported license.

The Stolpersteines are now the largest memorial project in the world.

The memorial plaques have been set for many groups of victims of the Nazis. They include Jewish people, Black people, Catholics opposed to the Nazis, disabled people, homosexual people, Jehovah's Witnesses, Roma and political dissidents. They have also been made for inmates of concentration camps held and being transported in secret on SS Cap Arcona. On 3 May 1945 after the suicide of Hitler but 1 day before the surrender of German troops this and two other ships were attacked by the RAF in the mistaken belief that the ships held escaping Nazi leaders. There were 5,000 former concentration camp inmates aboard. Only 350 survived.

Gunter Demnig laying Stolpersteines (in Hamburg)

Image by Jürgen Howaldt Wikicommons Creative Commons Attribution-Share Alike 3.0 Germany license.

Klenze's Walhalla seen from the Danube.

The building was erected under the supervision of the architect Leo von Klenze. This was opened in 1842. The memorial was commissioned by King Ludwig I of Bavaria (1825-48) to give honour to distinguished people in German history. These distinguished people include politicians, sovereigns, scientists and artists. On display are 65 plaques and 130 busts covering 2,000 years of history.

Walhalla

Image W. Bulach Wikipedia the Creative Commons Attribution-Share Alike 4.0 International license.

Passau

Passau is known as the city of three rivers, the Danube is joined by the River Inn and the River Liz. The city has a population of about 50,000. It dates back to Roman times. It was once a well-known producer of swords and other bladed weapons.

In 1662 the city was rebuilt in the Baroque style after a devastating fire.

Passau Old town

Image Aconcagua Wikipedia Creative Commons license Attribution Generic disclosure Alike 3.0 license.

Adolf Hitler and his family lived in Passau for 2 years between 1892 and 1894. During World War II, the town also housed three sub-camps of the Mauthausen-Gusen concentration camp.

St Stephens Cathedral

Image by Aconcagua Wikipedia Creative Commons Attribution-Share Alike 3.0 Unported license.

The Baroque cathedral dates from 1688. There have been a number pf previous churches on this site. It has the largest church organ in the world, although the "organ" is really several separate organs of different tonal styles all accessible from one or more consoles.

St Stephens Cathedral

Image by s. somkuti Wikipedia the Creative Commons Attribution-Share Alike 2.0 Generic license.

Confluence of the three rivers, Passau

Image bk Wikipedia Creative Commons Attribution-Share Alike 2.0 Generic license.

Old Townhall, Passau

Image Aconcagua Wikipedia Creative Commons Attribution-Share Alike 3.0 Unported license.

The old town hall is on the bank of the Danube in the town square. Three buildings are associated, the Old Town Hall, the New Town Hall and the Old Main Customs Office. The old townhall dates from 1298 and has a 38 metre tower dating from 1889.

Veste Oberhaus fortress

Image by Aconcagua Creative Commons Attribution-Share Alike 3.0 Unported license.

The fortress dates from 1219 and overlooks Passau from its stance on a mountain crest. Once the building housed the Bishop of Passau. It is now a museum, a youth hostel, a restaurant, and an open-air theatre.

Salzburg

The city of Salzburg dates from Roman times around 15 BC. The name derives from the salt industry originating in the 8th century. Salzburg lies on the banks of the River Salzach. Baroque churches and other buildings are in abundance.

The occupation and annexation of Austria, the Anschluss, took place on 12 March 1938 and German troops moved into the city. Following this, political opposition members, Jewish citizens and other minorities were arrested and deported to concentration camps. The synagogue was destroyed. Russian prisoners were held here. During World War II thousands of houses were bombed and hundreds of inhabitants were killed by the Allied Forces. Half of the city buildings sustained severe damage, including the town's bridges and the dome of the cathedral. American forces entered the city on 5 May 1945.

Salzburg on the River Salzach

Residenzplatz

In the square in the old town are the New Residenz with its carillon, the Cathedral, the Old Residenz and the Residenz Fountain. Salzburg Residenz is the former residence of the Prince-Archbishops. In the Salzburg Residenz is the Residenzgalerie, a museum of art.

Salzburg Cathedral

Image by Mattana Wikipedia Creative Commons Attribution 2.0 Generic license.

The cathedral dates from 771 but has been rebuilt on several occasions. Salzburg Cathedral still contains the baptismal font in which composer Wolfgang Amadeus Mozart was baptized.

Hohensalzburg Fortress

This overlooks Salzburg and is one of the largest castles in Europe. It dates from 1077.

Hohensalzburg Fortress Funicular

Mirabell Palace and gardens

Mirabell Palace dates from 1606 and was built for prince-archbishop Wolf Dietrich for his beloved Salome Alt. It is now used for weddings and conferences. Mozart played music here.

Mozart House

Image by Andrew Bossi the Creative Commons Attribution-Share Alike 2.5 Generic license.

Mozart's house is on Makartplatz. Mozart and his family lived here between 1773 and 1787. It is known as the "Dance Master's House". This was destroyed in WW2 but has been reconstructed.

Mozart's birthplace

Image Elisa.rolle Wikipedia Creative Commons Attribution-Share Alike 4.0 International license.

Mulln Church

This church dates from the 15th century and is on the banks of the River Salzach.

Other sites to visit in Salzburg

Franciscan Church (Franziskanerkirche)

Holy Trinity Church (Dreifaltigkeitskirche)

Kollegienkirche

Nonnberg Abbey, a Benedictine monastery

St Peter's Abbey with the Petersfriedhof

Großes Festspielhaus

Getreidegasse

St. Sebastian's Church

Outside the Old Town

Schloss Hellbrunn Castle

Image by Nicholas Even Wikipedia Creative Commons Attribution-Share Alike 3.0 Unported license.

This dates from 1613. Schloss Hellbrunn is most known for its grounds and Trick Fountains.

Trick Fountains Schloss Hellbrunn Castle

Image by Matilda Wikipedia Creative Commons Attribution 3.0 Unported license.

Mention must be made of the film "The Sound of Music" that was largely filmed in Schloss Leopoldskron, a rococo palace and national historic monument in Leopoldskron-Moos, a southern district of Salzburg. It is possible to book tours of the various film locations in and around Salzburg.

Baroness Maria Augusta von Trapp DHS (1905- 1987) was the stepmother and matriarch of the Trapp Family Singers. She wrote The Story of the Trapp Family Singers, which was published in 1949 and was filmed as the 1956 West German film The Trapp Family. The Broadway musical The Sound of Music (1959) and its 1965 film version were based on her story.

Schloss Leopoldskron
Image Shearing Holidays Wikipedia Creative Commons Attribution 2.0 Generic license.

Schloss Leopoldskron Palace is built in a rococo style. It is situated on Leopoldskroner Weiher lake and has a 7 hectare parkland. It is now a private hotel. The palace dates from 1736.

In 1939 the palace was confiscated by the Germans as a national treasure during the taking of "Jewish property" throughout Austria. During the same year, Hermann Göring assigned the palace to Princess Stephanie von Hohenlohe, an Austrian who had been spying for the Nazis in Britain and Europe.

The palace sustained minor damage during the war.

In 1964, the film The Sound of Music, directed by Robert Wise and starring Julie Andrews, was produced in Salzburg in the grounds adjacent to those of Schloss Leopoldskron, which were used for outside scenes. The palace interior was never used in the film.

Two love scenes, one between Liesl and Rolf (featuring the song Sixteen Going on Seventeen) and the other between Maria and the Captain (Something Good) were filmed in a gazebo on a film stage. Only long shots of the Austrian gazebo are seen in the film. This gazebo is now in the Hellbrunn Palace.

The Salzburg Festival

The Salzburg Festival of music was established in 1920. This also featured in the film The Sound of Music. During the Anschluss in 1938 the Nazi regime caused severe effects on the festival. Toscanini resigned in protest, Jewish musicians such as Reinhardt and Georg Solti emigrated. The festival continued until 1944 when Joseph Goebbels caused it to be cancelled. Immediately after the Allied victory the festival started again.

Notable composers and musician connected to Salzburg

Wolfgang Amadeus Mozart was born in Salzburg. His family is buried in a graveyard in the old town

Johann Michael Haydn, the brother of Joseph Haydn and the orchestral conductor **Herbert von Karajan** were born in Salzburg.

Linz

Linz is the third largest city in Austria and has a population of about 200,000. Founded by the Romans it was originally named *Lentia*. The name Linz was first recorded in AD 799.

The mathematician Kepler was once a resident here. The local university is named after him. The composer Anton Bruckner worked here as an organist in the Old Cathedral.

Adolf Hitler moved to Linz to live when a child as did Adolf Eichmann. Twelve miles from Linz was the Mauthausen-Gusen concentration camp. The city of Linz has made huge moves to confront its past with the Nazis. Many streets have been renamed and many memorials erected.

Hauptplatz (main Square) Linz and Plague column

Image Tocfo Wikipedia Creative Commons Attribution-Share Alike 3.0 Austria license.

This very large main square dates from 1230. Around the square are many buildings including the Old Town Hall and the Feichtinger House with its famous carillon. To the west is the old town with Renaissance and Baroque buildings.

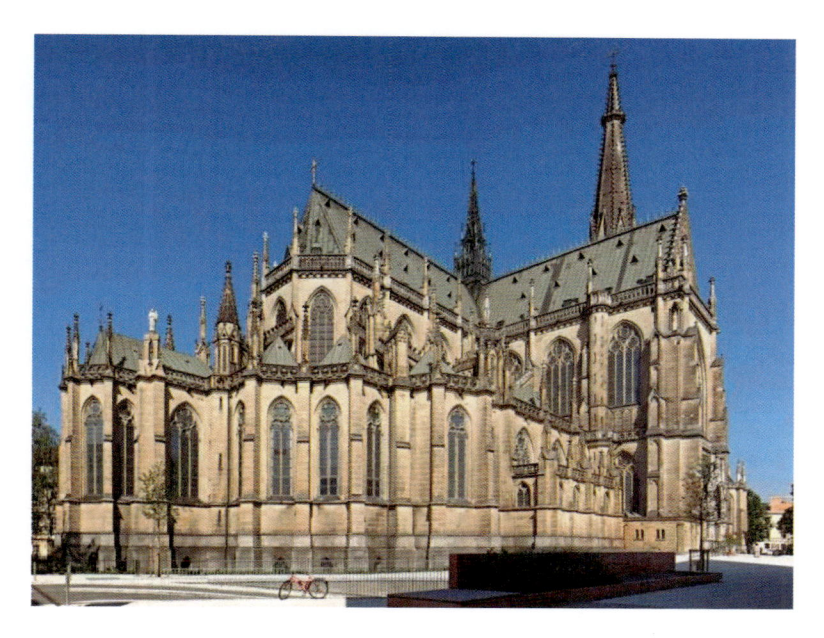

St. Mary's Cathedral, Linz

Image Pierre Bona Wikipedia Creative Commons Attribution-Share Alike 3.0 Unported.

St. Mary's Roman Catholic Cathedral dates from 1862 and is built from sandstone. It has exceptionally fine stained-glass windows dating from 1868. One window, the Linz Window, depicts the history of Linz, including Beethoven, Buchner and Kepler and important scenes and buildings of Linz.

St. Mary's Cathedral, Linz

Image Andrzej Otrębski Wikipedia Creative Commons Attribution-Share Alike 4.0 International license.

The Linz Window

Image Dieringer63 Creative Commons Attribution-Share Alike 4.0 International license.

It has exceptionally fine stained-glass windows dating from 1868, including the Linz Window, which depicts the history of Linz, including Beethoven, Buchner and Kepler and important scenes and buildings of Linz. Many stained-glass windows sustained severe war damage in WW2.

Mozarthaus

Image Christian Wirth Wikipedia Creative Commons Attribution-Share Alike 3.0 Unported license.

Mozart stayed in this renaissance house in November 1783. Here Mozart composed his Linz Symphony and his Linz Sonata taking only three days to do so. He was a guest of the Count of Thun.

The Brucknerhaus

Image by NeoUrfahraner Wikipedia the Creative Commons Attribution-Share Alike 3.0 Unported license.

This concert hall in Linz is named after Anton Bruckner. It opened in 1974. It contains three concert halls, the largest being the Bruckner Hall.

Museum of Dentistry (Zahnmuseum)

Image Christian Wirth Wikipedia Attribution-ShareAlike 3.0 Unported.

This museum illustrates the development of dentistry with an exhibition of equipment used in dentistry from the early 18th century to the recent past. Among the exhibits is a picture of St. Apollonia, patron saint of dentists. When it was demanded that she renounce her beliefs her teeth were broken and she was burned at the stake. She is said to have stated that all toothache sufferers who asked for her help would be released from their grief.

Johannes Kepler Observatory:

Image Raab Wikipedia Creative Commons Attribution-Share Alike 4.0 International license.

This opened in 1983. It has a computer controlled Cassegrain mirror telescope, which has a main mirror with a 500mm aperture and a focal length of 5m. Lectures on astronomy are held here.

Melk

Melk in the heart of the wine region, lies on the Danube. It has a population of about 5000 and has a history dating from about the year 831. High up above the city on a rock outcrop stands Melk Abbey, a 900 year old Italian baroque Benedictine monastery.

Melk Abbey

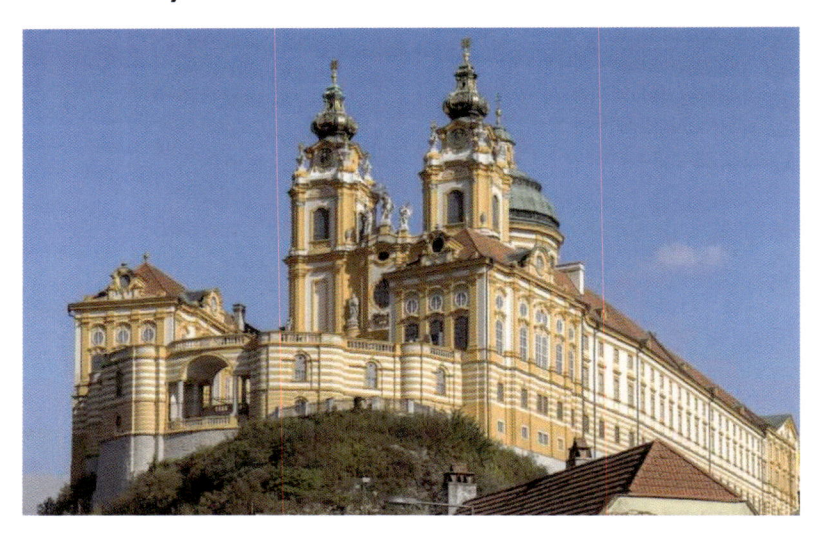

Image Thomas Ledl Wikipedia Creative Commons Attribution-Share Alike 4.0 International license.

The Abbey from the Danube

Image Uoaei1 Wikipedia Creative Commons Attribution-Share Alike 4.0 International license.

The Abbey was built on the site of a pre-existing castle its history dates from 1089. In the 12th century a monastery was founded here. The present structure of the Abbey dates from 1702. The church was designed by the architect Jakob Prandtauer (1660-1726). The abbey church frescos are by Johann Michael Rottmayr. The library contains medieval manuscripts and a collection of musical manuscripts and frescos by Paul Troger.

Melk Abbey

Prelate's courtyard

Ceiling painting of the Marble Hall by Paul Troger

Image Alberto Fernandez Fernandez Wikipedia Creative Commons Attribution-Share Alike 3.0 Unported license.

The abbey contains the tomb of Saint Coloman of Stockerau and the remains of several members of the House of Babenberg, Austria's first ruling dynasty. The abbey suffered serious fire damage in 1974 following which restoration occurred, with work being done on the nave, the marble hall and various frescos.

In "The Name of the Rose" by Umberto Eco, the abbey is mentioned for one of the main characters, "Adso of Melk".

The Church

Image David Monniaux Wikipedia Creative Commons Attribution-Share Alike 3.0 Unported license.

The Library

Image Emgonzalez Wikipedia in the public domain

The Marble Hall

Image Vitold Muratov Wikipedia Creative Commons Attribution-Share Alike 4.0 International license.

Other sites to visit in Melk

The Forsthaus, which accommodates the city archives.

The Zaglauergasse and remnants of the city wall.

The Rathausplatz with a wood and copper entrance door.

The old bread store.

The 15th century Haus am Stein ('house at the rock') is the oldest building of Melk.

The Old Post Office, dating from 1792.

In the vicinity is a subcamp of the Mauthausen concentration camp complex. This had a gas chamber and crematorium. It is now a museum and is the present site of the Birago barracks of the Austrian Army. Over 10,000 people were killed here in the Holocaust.

Wachau Valley

The Wachau Valley lies along the Danube between Melk and Krems. It is a picturesque tourist destination. It is 36 kilometres in length and is noted as a wine region for dry Rieslings and Grüner Veltliners wines grown on the steep sides of the river. Along this part of the Danube can be seen castles, castle ruins and churches. Lying on the Danube in the valley is Dürnstein. One can cycle down the riverbanks here. The ride being a gentle downhill ride taking about 4 hours.

Schönbühel Castle sits on the Danube's south bank between Melk and Willendorf.

This 12th century castle lies 40 metres above the river.

Willendorf

In Willendorf the famous "Venus of Willendorf" from 30000 BCE was discovered. This is now in the natural history museum in Vienna. A copy can be found in Willendorf.

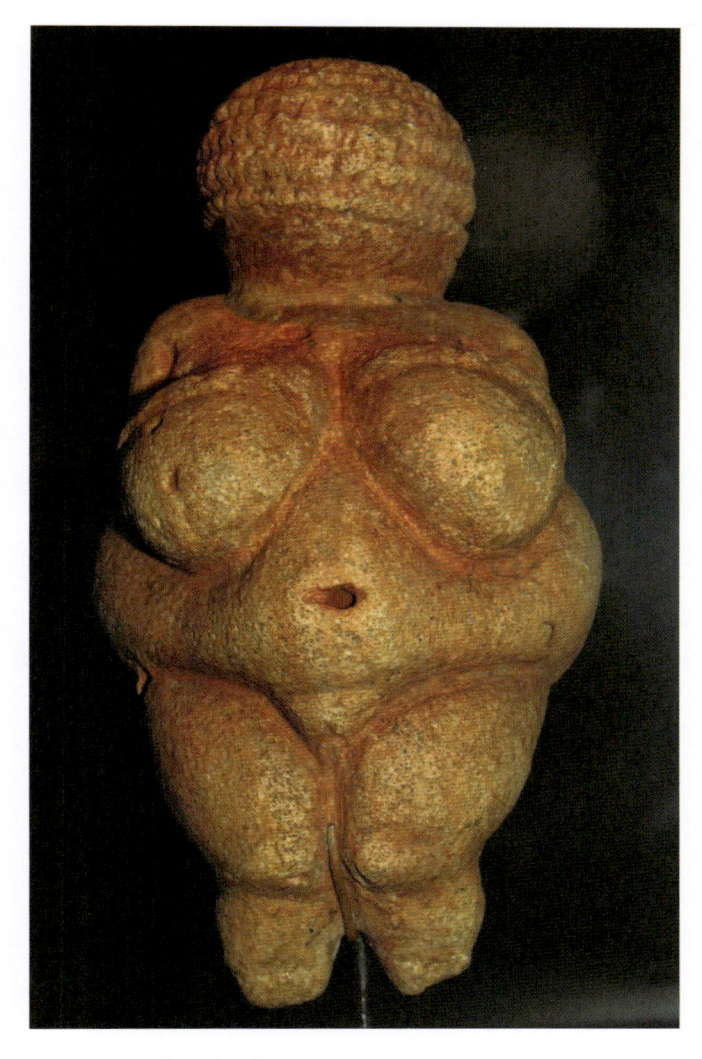

Venus von Willendorf

Image by Don Hitchcock Wikipedia Creative Commons Attribution-Share Alike 3.0 Unported license.

Hinterhaus Castle Ruins

These castle ruins are nearly one thousand-year old. It has Gothic bulwark and Renaissance fortifications. It is divided into three parts, the northwest lower altitudes bailey or courtyard; the main castle, and; the southwestern outer bailey. The castle was used in the 14th century by the Knights of Spitz.

The Late Gothic church of St. Maurice, Spitz

This 15th century church has an organ loft with statues of Christ and his apostles (1420) and an altarpiece (1799) depicting the martyrdom of St Maurice.

Church of Saint Rupert, Hofarnsdorf

The 15th century church has a medieval churchyard wall. It has a late Gothic pseudo-basilica.

Wehrkirche St. Michael

Wehrkirche St. Michael

This is a Roman Catholic fortified church of St. Michael. It is situated on a Celtic sacrificial site. It has a history dating back to the year 800 AD. It has a round defense tower. The tower is crowned by round arched battlements.

Between the apse of the fortified church and the fortified tower on the southeast corner of the fortifications is the Karner dating from 1395. This is a tall narrow building with stepped strong buttresses and two-lobed pointed arch windows.

Parish church of the Assumption of Mary at Weißenkirchen

The river here may be crossed by a ferry that can carry foot passengers, bicycles, motorcycles, and automobiles.

Weißenkirchen translates into English as 'white church'. The town dates from the 9th century.

The Gothic Pfarrkirche Mariae Himmelfahrt (Church of the Assumption of Mary) dates from the 14th century. It is surrounded by watchtowers and a defensive wall. The small tower dates from 1330 and is the original tower. The larger tower was built in 1531 as a defense against Turkish invaders. The interior of the church is late Gothic and Baroque.

Dürnstein

The picturesque town of Dürnstein lies on the Danube in the Wachau Valley. It is in the wine area and is a popular tourist destination. The history of the town dates from 1192.

The Castle in Dürnstein

This castle was where Richard the Lionheart was imprisoned in the 12th century by Duke Leopold V the Virtuous. The castle was destroyed by Swedish troops in 1692.

Dürnstein

This is a popular touring area in the Wachau valley. The town is overlooked by its castle ruins. The building to the left of the above photograph is the Hotel Schloss. This was once a castle dating from 1622. It is flanked by two towers.

Dürnstein Abbey and the Blue Bell Tower of the Collegiate Church

The blue tower dates from 1773.

The Abbey

The Collegiate Church, Assumption of Mary

Image BWag Wikipedia Creative Commons Attribution-Share Alike 3.0 Unported license.

Dürnstein

The Danube at Dürnstein

Dürnstein

Dürnstein

Town Hall Courtyard, Dürnstein

In 1547, the Town Hall was set up in a late Gothic building in the town centre. A few years later it was renovated in the renaissance style.

Vienna

Vienna is the largest city in Austria with a population of about 2 million. It has become known as the City of Music, having played a leading role in classical music. Wolfgang Amadeus Mozart, Joseph Haydn, Ludwig van Beethoven, Franz Schubert, Johannes Brahms, Gustav Mahler and Arnold Schoenberg all worked here. Sigmund Freud the psychoanalyst lived here.

The city is encircled by the thoroughfare, the Ringstrasse. This was constructed in the mid-19th century. Large public buildings were erected along it in a variety of architectural styles, featuring Classical, Gothic, Renaissance and Baroque architecture. There are several named sections to this ring road:

Schottenring (named after the Schottenstift, a Roman Catholic monastery).

Universitätsring (university).

Dr.-Karl-Renner-Ring (Karl Renner), formerly Parlamentsring.

Burgring (Hofburg).

Opernring (Vienna State Opera).

Kärntner Ring (named after Kärntner Straße, the road that led south to Carinthia).

Schubertring (Franz Schubert).

Parkring (Wiener Stadtpark).

Stubenring (named after the Stubenbastei fortification, part of Vienna's city walls since 1156).

In 1938 Vienna became part of Nazi Germany. It remained so until 1945 when Russia, Britain and America regained the city from Germany. During this time a large number of private and public buildings sustained war damage.

It is not within the realm of this book to delve further into the history of Vienna. The author suggests that for further information a detailed guidebook is consulted.

Kunsthistorisches Museum

This is known as the Museum of Fine Art and is the largest museum in Austria. It has an octagonal dome. It stands on the Ringstraße. In the square opposite is the public Maria-Theresien-Platz and the Empress Maria Theresia monument.

Empress Maria Theresia Monument

Empress Maria Theresia was the only female ruler of the Habsburg dominions and the last of the House of Habsburg. For 40 years she was the sovereign of Austria, Hungary, Croatia, Bohemia, Transylvania, Mantua, Milan, Lodomeria and Galicia, the Austrian Netherlands, and Parma. The high reliefs are figures from the fields of politics, economics, and the arts, including Haydn, Gluck, and Mozart.

Vienna City Park

Image by Gryffindor Wikipedia Creative Commons Attribution-Share Alike 3.0 Unported license.

Äußeres Burgtor, the outer castle gate

Heldenplatz

The Heldenplatz is a public area situated in front of the Hofburg Palace. Adolf Hitler's ceremonial announcement of the Austrian Anschluss to Nazi Germany took place here on 15 March 1938.

Statue Archduke Charles on the Heldenplatz

Hofburg Imperial Palace

Hofburg Imperial Palace

The Swiss Gate

This was the original main gate.

St Stephens Cathedral

Image by BWag Wikipedia Creative Commons Attribution-Share Alike 4.0 International license.

This Romanesque and Gothic Roman Catholic Cathedral on Stephansplatz dates from 1359 in its present appearance. The main tower stands at 136 metres in height. The cathedral has an ornate coloured glazed tile roof. St. Stephen's Cathedral has 23 bells in total. It is said that Beethoven discovered the severity of his deafness when he saw birds flying out of the bell tower as a result of the bells' tolling but could not hear the bells.

St Stephens Cathedral

Image by BWag Wikipedia Creative Commons Attribution-Share Alike 4.0 International license.

State Opera House

Image by BWag Wikipedia Creative Commons Attribution-Share Alike 4.0 International license.

The building dates from 1861. It was severely damaged in WW2 along with the entire décor and props for more than 120 operas with around 150,000 costumes. Restoration over a prolonged period occurred. It is one of the busiest opera houses in the world producing 50 to 60 operas per year and ten ballet productions in more than 350 performances. The opera house employs over 1000 people and has a budget of 100 million euros with about 50% being subsidized by the state.

Burgtheatr

Image by MrPanyGoff Wikipedia the Creative Commons Attribution-Share Alike 3.0 Unported license.

This is also known as the Imperial Court Theatre. It dates from 1731. The theatre company consists of regular members who perform in a traditional style and speech typical of German language Burgtheater performances. It suffered war damage in 1945 and been completely restored. When under Nazi rule in 1943, an extreme antisemitic production of The Merchant of Venice was staged at the Burgtheater. This was made at the specific direction of Joseph Goebbels, the Reich Minister of Propaganda of Nazi Germany. Participating in this was the Nazi collaborator Werner Johannes Krauss. He also took part in the antisemitic propaganda film Jud Süß. This was considered to be one of the most antisemitic films of all time. The film was seen by 20 million people in Germany. Members of the SS and police were asked to watch the movie by Heinrich Himmler.

Town Hall (City Hall)

Image by Gryffindor Wikipedia Creative Commons Attribution-Share Alike 3.0 Unported license.

The City Hall dates from 1872 and was built in a Neo-Gothic style. On the top of the tower is the Rathausmann, a 5.4 metres tall iron standard-bearer.

Vienna

Vienna

Plague Column

Image Thomas Ledl Wikipedia Creative Commons Attribution-Share Alike 3.0 Austria license.

The Baroque memorial, the Plague Column or Trinity Column, is a Holy Trinity column located on the Graben. It was erected after the Great Plague epidemic in 1679.

The pedestal is for mankind in which the upper third Leopold I prays to God.

The middle third illustrates angels mediating between God and man.

At the top is the Holy Trinity.

St Peters Church from Graben Street

St Peters church is a Baroque Roman Catholic parish church. It dates from 1701 on the site of a medieval church building. It is situated on Petersplatz, next to Graben Street.

St Peters Church

Image by BWag Wikipedia Creative Commons Attribution-Share Alike 4.0 International license.

St. Francis of Assisi Church

This Catholic church dates from 1898. It is used by the Vienna English Speaking Catholic Community.

St. Francis of Assisi Church

Image BWag Wikipedia Creative Commons Attribution-Share Alike 3.0 Austria license.

The DC Tower, Donau City, Vienna

The Donau City Tower is 250 metres high. It opened in 2014, taking three years to complete. Two other towers, DC2 and 3 have not yet materialized. The tower houses a 5-star hotel, a fitness club and office accommodation. Nearby is the recently developed Copa Beach leisure area. The whole area was built on what was once a flood plain.

Copa Beach, Donau City

Copa Beach, Donau City

Bratislava

Bratislava is the capital of Slovakia. It has a population of just under half a million. The city was once called Pressburg. Many composers of music have had associations with Bratislava. Amongst these are Hummel who was born here, Joseph Haydn who was born nearby, Mozart gave his first public concert here when aged 6 years, Beethoven visited many times and his *Missa Solemnis* was performed here in 1835, Liszt played here on many occasions from the age of 9 years, Anton Rubenstein composed works here and Bella Bartok studied here.

Hviezdoslav Square and Slovak National Theatre

Image by Jorge Láscar Wikipedia Creative Commons Attribution 2.0 Generic license.

Hviezdoslav Square (Hviezdoslavovo námestie) is in the old town. It lies between the New Bridge and the Slovak National Theatre. It has a 1000 year history. The square is named after Pavol Országh Hviezdoslav (1849-1921), a Slovak poet, dramatist, translator, and for a short time, member of the Czechoslovak parliament. The most notable buildings are the Notre Dame cloister and today's Slovak National Theatre which can be found in the eastern part of square.

Hviezdoslav Square

Image by Jorge Láscar Wikipedia Creative Commons Attribution 2.0 Generic license.

Slovak National Theatre

Slovak National Theatre is a Neo-Renaissance theatre building in the Old Town of Bratislava. (There is now a new theatre near the Danube). The building dates from 1885 and is built on the site of a previous theatre building. The Ganymede Fountain stands in front of the theatre.

The Ganymede Fountain was the work of the Bratislava sculptor Viktor Oskar Tilgner (1844 -1896). On the day after completing a Mozart Sculpture in Vienna he died of a heart attack.

Main Square, the Old Town Hall and Jesuit Church

The old Town Hall dates from the 14th century with the tower being built in 1370. It was built by joining up several houses. It houses the city museum. It was also used in the past as a prison (the town dungeons can still be seen) and as a mint.

To the left of the town hall building is a Jesuit Church.

Roland fountain on the Main Square

The Roland Fountain is also known as the Maximilian Fountain. Maximilian II, the king of Royal Hungary in 1572 ordered the fountain as a source of water for the public. On top of the fountain is a statue of Maximilian as a knight in full armour.

The Ludovit Stur Monument

Ludovit Stur was involved in the revival of the Slovak language, a teacher, poet, philosopher and politician (he was also a member of the Hungarian parliament).

Cumil

This relatively new sculpture dates from 1997. Cumil, the sewer worker, is emerging from a sewer. The word Čumil translates as "The Watcher". The legend states that if you touch the top of his hat it brings you good luck and if you touch his nose it gives you fertility.

Schoener Naci

Image Henry Flower Wikipedia Creative Commons Attribution-Share Alike 3.0 Unported license.

Schöner Náci, also known as Ignac Lamar (1897-1967) was a shoemaker's son. He was the grandson of a clown. It is said that he was in love with a woman who did not return his love. He could often be seen giving flowers to women when he walked the streets of Bratislava. He used to walk the streets of the old town in top hat and tails. He received free food from several of the city's cafes and supported himself with occasional cleaning work.

The Church of St. Elizabeth

Image Fred Romero Wikipedia Creative Commons Attribution 2.0 Generic license.

The Church of St. Elizabeth is also known locally as The Blue Church. It is an Art Nouveau Catholic Church. It dates from 1909 and has one nave.

The Church of St. Elizabeth

Image RoyFocker Wikipedia in the public domain.

The Primates Castle

This is a neoclassical building dating from 1778. It was built for Archbishop József Batthyány. Its most famous chamber is the Hall of Mirrors, where council meetings are held. The President of Slovakia lived here for a short time until 1996.

In 1903, when reconstruction work was being carried out, six previously unknown tapestries dating from the 1630s were found behind a wall, depicting the legend of Hero and Leander and their tragic love.

17th century tapestry in The Primates Castle

Image Smuconlaw Wikipedia the Creative Commons Attribution-Share Alike 4.0 International license.

The tapestries were designed by Francis Cleyn (1582-1658). They were woven in Mortlake, London.

The Primates Castle interior

St. Michael's Gate

The St. Michaels Gate dates from about 1300. In 1758, the statue of St. Michael and the Dragon was placed on its top when the tower was rebuilt. The Exhibition of Weapons of Bratislava City Museum is to be found here. This was one of four fortified gates for entry to the city supported by city walls.

In the vicinity of the Primates Castle is the Hummel Museum.

Plaque in honour of Franz Liszt the composer on wall of Pauli Palace

Pauli Palace

Beethoven Apartments

Beethoven Apartments is in the Keglevičov palác. Here Beethoven gave music lessons and composed the Piano Sonata No. 4 in E-flat major, Op. 7 and the Piano Concerto No. 1 in C major, Op. 15. This and other piano sonatas were dedicated to his pupil Anna Louise Barbara Keglevich, also called Babetta.

The Mozart House

In 1762 six-year-old Wolfgang Amadeus Mozart performed at this Palffy family residence generally known today as the Mozart House.

The Bird Fountain

A drinking water fountain that is attended frequently by birds.

St Martins Gothic Cathedral

St Martins is a Roman Catholic cathedral that dates from 1311. The tower is topped by a gold-plated replica of the

Crown of St. Stephen and is 85 metres high. In 1760 the Gothic tower was hit by lightning and was rebuilt in the Baroque style. In 1835 this was destroyed by fire and had to be reconstructed in 1847. The nave consists of three aisles divided by two rows of eight columns.

Adjacent is a monument to a synagogue, a neighboring building for centuries. In 1970 the Communist government demolished it when the new Nový Most bridge was constructed.

St Martins Cathedral

St Martins Cathedral

St. Martins Cathedral, Stained Glass Window

New Nový Most Bridge

The Holocaust Memorial, Bratislava

The Holocaust Memorial erected in 1996 is located in the Old Town. It was here that the Rybné Square Synagogue was demolished in 1969. This monument was erected in 1996 to commemorate the 105,000 Holocaust victims from Slovakia. It is a memorial both to Holocaust victims and to the Neolog Synagogue destroyed in the Soviet period.

The sculpture is an abstract representation. It stands on a black granite platform inscribed with the words

"Zachor" ("Remember" in Hebrew) and "Pamätaj" ("Remember" in Slovak).

Atop stands the Star of David.

Neologická synagogue, Bratislava
Image from an old postcard, 1914. Image Wikicommons in the public domain.

Neologická synagogue in the 1960s, Bratislava

Image Zdenka Vopatova Wikicommons Creative Commons Attribution-Share Alike 4.0 International license.

The name Neologická refers to it being a Reform Synagogue.

The Synagogue was built in 1893 from a design by architect Dezso Milch. It was a rectangular building and had an organ. The Synagogue contained oriental motifs and decorations. The western façade was in Moorish style with two towers on the corners. These were octagonal and had domed roofs. In the middle of the facade there were 5 entrances, which formed Moorish arches. The Synagogue sustained no damage in WW2. There was an intention to convert it into a Jewish museum. The Synagogue was demolished between 1967 and 1969.

Hrad Castle

Hrad Castle

Image LMih Wikipedia Creative Commons Attribution-Share Alike 3.0 Unported license.

This castle overlooks the town from the top of a rocky hill. It dates from the 9th century. After falling into ruin, restoration was started in 1957.

Mirbach Palace

Image Dguendel Wikipedia Creative Commons Attribution 3.0 Unported license.

The Rococo Mirbach Palace dates from 1768. It was named for a past owner, Count Emil Mirbach. He was shot by the invading Russians in 1945 who took over his castle and contents. The building now holds the Bratislava City Gallery.

Budapest

Budapest is the capital of Hungary and dates from 1873. The 19th century Chain Bridge over the Danube connects the hilly Buda district with the flat Pest district. Budapest was formed by uniting three cities, Buda, Óbuda, and Pest.

The Chain Bridge

The Chain Bridge

The bridge was designed by English engineer William Tierney Clark and was built by Scottish engineer Adam Clark. It dates from 1849.

Parliament building

The Parliament building dates from 1902. It is on the Pest side of the city and on the banks of the Danube. Designed by the Hungarian architect Imre Steindl, it is in the neo-Gothic style. The building can be viewed by visitors. On the side away from the Danube is Kossuth Lajos Square.

Parliament building, Debating chamber

Image Alex Prolmos Wikipedia Creative Commons Attribution 2.0 Generic license.

Parliament building, Main Staircase

Parliament building from Kossuth Lajos Square

The square was named in 1927 in honor of Lajos Kossuth. The square is surrounded by large public buildings. In the centre is a park, sculptures, and a memorial to the victims of the Kossuth Tér massacre on 25 October 1956.

Museum of Ethnography, Kossuth Lajos Square

The museum exhibits a collection of Hungarian folk objects dating from the 19th century. The collection includes pieces from everyday Hungarian life from before World War II, including pottery, costumes, boats, and furniture.

Ministry of Agriculture, Kossuth Lajos Square

This building faces parliament building in the square. On the wall can be seen bullet marks from the 1956 Hungarian Revolution against Soviet control.

On October 25th 1956, Soviet troops and state secret police fired on a crowd numbering several thousand. They took shelter behind the façade of the building. Up to 100 people were killed. Today, dozens of bronze balls, each only slightly smaller than a tennis ball, mark the site.

Lajos Kossuth monument, Kossuth Lajos Square

Count Gyula Andrássy statue, Kossuth Lajos Square

Count Gyula Andrássy was Hungary's prime minister between 1867 and 1871 and later foreign minister.

The Shoes Memorial on the Danube Bank

Can Togay, film director, created this memorial on the east bank of the Danube River with sculptor Gyula Pauer. It was made to honour thousands of Jews, who were killed by fascist Arrow Cross militiamen in Budapest during World War between II December 1944 and January 1945. They were ordered to take off their shoes and were shot at the edge of the water so that their bodies fell into the river and were carried away. The shoes were considered valuable and could be reused or traded. People who visit the memorial sometimes light candles or leave behind flowers. The sculptor created sixty pairs of shoes out of iron and these were attached to the stone embankment. It is situated near to the Parliament House.

Buda Castle

Image Dennis Jarvis Wikipedia the Creative Commons Attribution-Share Alike 2.0 Generic license.

The castle and palace complex of the Hungarian kings in Budapest dates from 1265. The present Baroque palace dates from 1749. The castle now houses the Hungarian National Gallery and the Budapest History Museum. The surrounding immediate area has many medieval, Baroque and Neoclassical houses, churches, public buildings and monuments.

A funicular links the castle to the Chain Bridge.

Fisherman's Bastion

This is an 140 metre long complex by the castle. It has seven stone towers that symbolize the seven chieftains of the Hungarians who founded Hungary in 895. It dates from 1895 and is built in a Neo-Romanesque style. The Fisherman's Bastion was severely damaged during the sieges of World War II. Restoration was completed in 1953.

Monument to Saint Stephen I

Saint Stephen I was the first king of Hungary. The statue is by the Fisherman's Bastion.

Matthias Church

This is a Roman Catholic church and is also known as the Church of the Assumption of the Buda Castle. The church dates from 1015 when it was built in a Romanesque style. It was rebuilt in late Gothic style in the second half of the 14th century and underwent restoration in the late 19th century.

Matthias Church

Image by D4m1en Wikipedia Creative Commons Attribution-Share Alike 3.0 Unported license.

Plague Tower

Image Mstyslav Chernov Wikipedia Creative Commons Attribution-Share Alike 4.0 International license.

This stands outside Matthias Church. The column commemorates those who died from two outbreaks of the Black Plague in 1691 and 1709.

Buda Tunnel

The Várhegy Tunnel or the Buda Castle Tunnel is a 350 metre long tunnel. It connects the Buda side of the Chain Bridge to Krisztinaváros. Arch.

Heroes' Square

Image Andrew Shiva Wikicommons CC BY-SA 4.0

This large public area is a statue complex featuring the Seven chieftains of the Magyars and other important Hungarian national leaders. The Millennium Monument overlooks the area. The inscription on the monument states:

"To the memory of the heroes who gave their lives for the freedom of our people and our national independence."

The Museum of Fine Arts and the Palace of Art are in the vicinity. Behind the monument are two matched colonnades, each with seven statues representing great figures of Hungarian history.

The left Collonade

Vajdahunyad Castle

Image Marc Ryckaert Wikipedia the Creative Commons Attribution 3.0 Unported license.

The castle dates from 1896. It was constructed to celebrate 1000 years in Hungary since the Hungarian Conquest of the Carpathian Basin in 895. It features copies of different buildings in Hungary. It thus features several different architectural styles: Romanesque, Gothic, Renaissance, and Baroque. Originally it was built from cardboard and wood but in 1904 it was rebuilt in stone and brick. The Museum of Hungarian Agriculture is in this building.

Synagogue and the Hungarian Jewish Museum

Image 2jaipm Wikipedia Creative Commons Attribution-Share Alike 4.0 International license.

Guided tours are available to see the interior of this Synagogue which is the largest synagogue in Europe. It is a reform Synagogue and can seat 3000 people.

The building dates from 1854 and was built in the Moorish Revival style. It consists of three aisles and two balconies. The ark contains various Torah scrolls taken from other synagogues that were destroyed during the Holocaust. The upper gallery has seating for women.

Dohány Street on which the Synagogue stands was on the border of the Jewish Ghetto.

This Synagogue contains an organ, an unusual addition. Franz Liszt and Camille Saint-Saëns played the original 5,000-pipe organ built in 1859. The present organ dates from 1996.

THE END

Printed in Great Britain
by Amazon